# Bond

# Assessment Papers

## Starter papers in
## English

### Sarah Lindsay

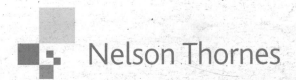

Nelson Thornes

First published in 2002 by:
Nelson Thornes Ltd

This edition published in 2007 by:
Nelson Thornes Ltd
Delta Place
27 Bath Road
CHELTENHAM
GL53 7TH
United Kingdom

08 09 10 11 / 10 9 8 7 6 5 4 3

A catalogue record for this book is available from the British Library

ISBN 978 0 7487 8497 4

Illustrations by Louise Barton
Page make-up by GreenGate Publishing Services, Tonbridge, Kent

Printed and bound in Croatia by Zrinski

## Acknowledgements

The authors and publishers wish to thank the following for permission
to use copyright material:

Jenny Dale for material from *2001 – A Space Oddity*; Peter Dixon for
*Magic Cat*; David Harmer for *Slick Nick's Dog's Tricks*; Trevor Harvey for
*My Eyes Are Watering*; *Hippo and Monkey* by John Jackman from *Collins
Primary Comprehension: Introductory Book*, Reprinted by permission of
HarperCollins Publishers Ltd; Kingfisher Publications Plc for material from
*The Kingfisher Nursery Library: Billy Goats Gruff and Other Stories*, retold
by Susan Price. Copyright © Susan Price 1992; Judith Nicholls for *The
Lion and the Mouse* Copyright © Judith Nicholls 2000; *Lucy and Tom's
1 2 3* by Shirley Hughes Copyright © Shirley Hughes, 1987 Reproduced
by permission of Penguin books Ltd; Steve Parker for material from *Learn
about the body*; Jo Peters for *My Hands*; *Hare and the Easter Eggs* by
Alison Uttley, Reprinted by permission of HarperCollins Publishers Ltd.
© (Alison Uttley) (1952); extract from *George Starts School* from *Philibert
the First and Other Stories*, by Dick King-Smith (1994), reprinted by
permission of A P Watt Ltd on behalf of Fox Busters Ltd.

Every effort has been made to trace the copyright holders, but if any
have been inadvertently overlooked the publishers will be pleased to
make the necessary arrangement at the first opportunity.

## Before you get started

## What is Bond?

This book is part of the Bond Assessment Papers series for English, which provides **thorough and continuous practice of key English skills** from ages five to thirteen. Bond's English resources are ideal preparation for many different kinds of tests and exams – from SATs to 11+ and other secondary school selection exams.

## What does this book cover?

It practises comprehension, spelling, grammar, punctuation and vocabulary work appropriate for children of this age. It is fully in line with the National Curriculum for English and the National Literacy Strategy. One of the key features of Bond Assessment Papers is that each one practises **a wide variety of skills and question types** so that children are always challenged to think – and don't get bored repeating the same question type again and again. We think that variety is the key to effective learning. It helps children 'think on their feet' and cope with the unexpected.

The age given on the cover is for guidance only. As the papers are designed to be reasonably challenging for the age group, any one child may naturally find him or herself working above or below the stated age. The important thing is that children are always encouraged by their performance. Working at the right level is the key to this.

## What does the book contain?

- **20 papers** – each one contains 20 questions.

- **Scoring devices** – there are score boxes in the margins and a Progress Chart at the back. The chart is a visual and motivating way for children to see how they are doing. Encouraging them to colour in the chart as they go along and to try to beat their last score can be highly effective!

- **Next Steps** – advice on what to do after finishing the papers can be found on the inside back cover.

- **Answers** – located in an easily-removed central pull-out section. If you lose your answers, please email cservices@ nelsonthornes.com for another copy.

- **Key English words** – on page 1 you will find a glossary of special key words that are used in the papers. These are highlighted in bold each time that they appear. These words are now used in the English curriculum and children are expected to know them at this age.

# How can you use this book?

One of the great strengths of Bond Assessment Papers is their flexibility. They can be used at home, school and by tutors to:

- provide regular English practice in **bite-sized chunks**
- **highlight strengths and weaknesses** in the core skills
- identify **individual needs**
- set **homework**
- set **timed formal practice** tests – allow about 25 minutes.

It is best to start at the beginning and work though the papers in order.

# What does a score mean and how can it be improved?

If children colour in the Progress Chart on page 44, this will give an idea of how they are doing. The Next Steps inside the back cover will help you to decide what to do next to help a child progress. We suggest that it is always valuable to go over any wrong answers with children.

# Don't forget the website...!

Visit www.assessmentpapers.co.uk for lots of advice, information and suggestions on everything to do with Bond, helping children to do their best, and exams.

# Key words

Some special words are used in this book. You will find them in **bold** each time they appear in the Papers. These words are explained here.

| | |
|---|---|
| **alphabetical order** | words arranged in the order found in the alphabet |
| **antonym** | a word with a meaning opposite to another word *hot – cold* |
| **compound word** | a word made up of two other words *football* |
| **consonant letters** | all letters of the alphabet apart from a, e, i, o, u (vowel letters) |
| **noun** | a word for somebody or something |
| **past tense** | something that has already happened |
| **plural** | more than one *cats* |
| **prefix** | a group of letters put at the beginning of a word *un*, *dis* |
| **present tense** | something happening now |
| **pronoun** | a word often put in place of a noun |
| **proper noun** | the name of a person, place, etc. *Ben* |
| **suffix** | a group of letters put at the end of a word *ly*, *ful* |
| **synonym** | a word with a very similar meaning to another word *quick – fast* |
| **verb** | a 'doing' or 'being' word |
| **vowel letters** | the letters a, e, i, o, u |

Today is Saturday. No school this morning! Lucy's clothes are on the chair in Mum and Dad's bedroom: a vest and pants, a pair of red socks, a T-shirt with stripes (first a red stripe, then a blue one, then a green), a skirt and, last of all, a pair of navy-blue shoes with red laces.

Lucy can put them all on by herself, all except for tying the laces, that is. Tom can put on his pants, one leg into each hole. But he needs a bit of help with his sweater. Which is the way out? It's all dark inside! At last he finds both the arm-holes and then out pops his head.

As soon as they are dressed Lucy and Tom go to see how Mopsa the cat is getting on. A very exciting thing happened a few weeks ago. Mopsa had kittens! She and her family are living in a box in the corner of the kitchen. It's very cosy inside with a bit of Lucy's old woolly blanket for a bed.

From *Lucy and Tom's 1 2 3* by Shirley Hughes

Underline the right answers.

1 What colour are Lucy's socks?

(red, blue, green)

2 What piece of clothing can Tom put on without help?

(socks, pants, sweater)

2

Answer these questions.

3 Who do Lucy and Tom go and see as soon as they are dressed?

_____

4 What makes Mopsa's box 'very cosy'?

_____

2

Circle the **vowel letters** in each word.

**5** p l a y                                    **6** h u n t

**7–8** d o n k e y                                                        ◯ 4

Copy each sentence. Put in the missing capital letters.

**9** we are going on holiday today.

_____

**10** the snow covered the playground.

_____

**11** harry runs very fast.

_____

**12** the dog ran after the ball.

_____                                         ◯ 4

Fill in the missing letters.

**13** d e f _____ h i

**14** t _____ v w x y

**15** l m _____ o p

**16** q r s _____ u                                                     ◯ 4

Underline the **nouns** in these sentences.

**17** I bumped my head.

**18** We enjoyed playing on the seesaw.

**19–20** The boy dropped his book.                                        ◯ 4

# Paper 2

## My Hands

Think of all my hands can do,
pick up a pin and do up a shoe,
they can help, they can hurt too,
or paint a summer sky bright blue.

They can throw and they can catch.
They clap the team that wins the match.
If I'm rough my hands can scratch.
If I'm rude my hands can snatch.

Gently, gently they can stroke,
carefully carry a glass of Coke,
tickle my best friend for a joke,
but I won't let them nip and poke.

My hands give and my hands take.
With Gran they bake a yummy cake.
They can mend but they can break.
Think of music hands can make.

By Jo Peters

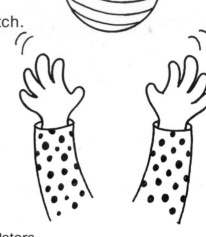

Underline the right answers.

1 What do the hands in the poem paint?

(a shoe, a pin, a sky)

2 What do the hands in the poem do if they are rude?

(catch, scratch, snatch)

2

Answer these questions.

3 What do the hands in the poem do with Gran?

_____

4 Write about something your hands did this morning.

_____

2

Write a word that rhymes with the word in **bold**.

5 hen    _____

6 book    _____

7 bell    _____

8 jump    _____

◯ 4

Copy each sentence. Add the missing full stops.

9 The stars shone brightly in the sky

_____

10 Dan ran home as fast as he could

_____

11 The children played in the park

_____

12 Ahmed finished his homework

_____

◯ 4

Underline the **proper nouns**.

13–16

David        nest        banana

goat       Tuesday       kite       London

gate       bridge       Scotland

◯ 4

Write a word with *sh* to match each picture.

17

_____

18

_____

19

_____

20

_____

◯ 4

## Paper 3

**Printing with paint**

You will need:

- some thin sponge
- a felt-tip pen
- some glue
- a square piece of cardboard
- some thick paint
- a large piece of paper

**1** Draw a simple shape on a piece of thin sponge using a felt-tip pen.

**2** Cut out your shape carefully and stick it with glue on a square piece of cardboard to make a print block. Wait until the glue dries.

**3** Cover the sponge on your print block with thick paint. Press the block on your piece of paper a number of times. When the paint on the sponge runs out, you can add more to continue printing.

You can make other printing blocks using different shapes cut out of thin sponge, or string dipped in glue and left to dry.

Underline the right answers.

1  What type of paint do you need to print with?

(thin, thick, doesn't matter)

2  When do you add more paint to the sponge?

(each time you print, never, when the paint runs out)

Answer these questions.

3  When you stick the sponge to the cardboard you should wait until the glue dries. Why do you think this is?

_____

4  Write what you think you could use your printed paper for.

_____

2

2

6

Read these sentences. Write whether they happened in the **past** or are happening in the **present**.

5 Shona jumped into the puddle. _____

6 Manjit is flying his kite. _____

7 Kate walked home from school. _____

8 Elias is playing the drums. _____ ○ 4

Write an **antonym** (a word with the opposite meaning) for each of these words.

9 long _____     10 hot _____

11 wet _____     12 in _____ ○ 4

Put the words in the right rhyming set.

13–18

spoon     loot     noon     tool

stool     boot

| root | pool | moon |
|------|------|------|
|      |      |      |
|      |      |      |

○ 6

Write two simple sentences about your school.

19 _____

20 _____ ○ 2

# Paper 4

Once upon a time, there was an old woman who was baking. She made a gingerbread man for tea. She cut him out of spicy gingerbread and gave him currants for his eyes and mouth and currant buttons down his front. Then she put him in the oven to bake.

A little while later, there was a knock at the door. Not the kitchen door – the oven door! A voice shouted, "Let me out! Let me out!" So the old woman opened the oven door and *whoosh*! the gingerbread man raced past her, across the kitchen floor and out into the garden. The old woman ran after him shouting, "Come back! I baked you for tea!"

But the gingerbread man only laughed and ran on, calling, "Run, run, as fast as you can – you won't catch me, I'm the gingerbread man!"

From *The Gingerbread Man* retold by Susan Price

Underline the right answers.

1 Which meal was the old woman making the gingerbread man for?

(breakfast, lunch, tea)

2 On which door did the gingerbread man knock?

(the kitchen door, the oven door, the front door)

2

Answer these questions.

3 Where did the gingerbread man go after he left the kitchen?

_____

4 Write the reason you think the gingerbread man ran away.

_____

2

Write a question for each statement.

Example    Sarah had baked beans for tea.

*What did Sarah have for tea?*

5  Statement:  Helen is seven years old.

_____

6  Statement:  Tim went swimming after school.

_____

7  Statement:  Liam rode his bike to Tom's.

_____    **3**

Write the **plural** of each word.

8  window  _____    9  swan  _____

10  train  _____    11  sister  _____

12  book  _____    **5**

Underline the **verb** in each sentence.

13  Stuart jumped off the wall.

14  We ran quickly through the forest.

15  Iona sat on the comfortable chair.

16  They swam to the other side of the river.    **4**

Finish the sentences.

The Lewis family live in Hull. Gareth is Alice's brother. Their mother, a kind lady called Karen, helps at the local nursery. David, their father, works in the local supermarket.

17  David is Alice's f_____.

18  Karen is Gareth's m_____.

19  Alice is Gareth's s_____.

20  Gareth is Alice's b_____.    **4**

# Paper 5

**Your pet rabbit**

Rabbits are usually friendly animals. You can get big rabbits, and small ones called dwarf rabbits. Some have ears that stand up straight and others have lop ears. They are easy pets to keep but must be kept clean and always have food and water available.

**Looking after your rabbit**

Every day your pet rabbit needs to be given fresh dried food and fresh water. They enjoy nibbling hay which can be bought from your local pet shop. If your rabbit lives in a hutch and doesn't have a run it is important to give it some greens from the garden. Rabbits particularly enjoy dandelion leaves. Rabbits need their hutches to be cleaned out regularly. They need clean sawdust or straw. No animal likes sleeping in a dirty bed!

**Watch out!**

The claws and teeth of rabbits can sometimes grow too long. If this ever happens, take your rabbit to the vet and they will trim them for you. If you don't, it could be very painful for your rabbit.

Always be careful as some rabbits are very clever at escaping and when they get out they can run very fast!

Underline the right answers.

1–2 What two things must rabbits always have available?

(food, a plastic dish, water, a brush)

3 Where should you take your rabbit if its claws grow too long?

(the garden, a pet shop, the vet)

**3**

Answer these questions.

4 What do rabbits particularly enjoy eating?

_____

5 Why is it important to clean out your rabbit's hutch regularly?

_____

**2**

Fill the gaps correctly with *was* or *were*.

   **6** The dog _____ taken for a walk.

   **7** The children _____ riding the ponies.

   **8** There _____ lots of swans on the river.

   **9** Leena _____ cooking a cake.

4

Copy the sentences and add the missing capital letters and full stops.

   **10** the rain soaked the children

   _____

   **11** the park was very busy

   _____

   **12** two ducks played in the water

   _____

3

Answer these questions.

   **13** What colour is a post-box?          _____

   **14** What colour is grass?               _____

   **15** What colour is a carrot?            _____

   **16** What colour is a buttercup?         _____

4

Look at the picture and write four words with *ar*.

   **17** _____          **18** _____

   **19** _____          **20** _____

4

*Now go to the Progress Chart to record your score!*     Total     20

### My Eyes are Watering

I've got a cold
And that is why
My eyes are watering.

It's nothing to do
With getting caught
When I planned
To SMASH
The rounders ball
SO FAR
That it would go
Into PERMANENT ORBIT
Round the school.
It would've done, too –
If Lucy Smith
Hadn't RUSHED
To catch it.

'Look at Trevor –
He's having a cry!'
Not true.
I've got a cold
And THAT is why
My eyes are watering.

OK?

By Trevor Harvey

Underline the right answers.

**1** What game was Trevor playing?

(football, rounders, netball)

**2** How did Trevor plan to hit the ball?

(a smash high in the air, a smash along the ground,
a smash behind him)

2

Answer these questions.

**3** Who caught the ball Trevor hit?

_____

**4** Do you think Trevor really had a cold? Why?

_____  ⟨ 2

Underline the **nouns**.

**5–8** build    tasty    hand    table    dirty    sausage    write    kite    ○ 4

Do the word sums. Write the **compound words**.

**9** tooth      +      brush      =      _____

**10** basket    +      ball        =      _____

**11** lunch     +      time        =      _____

**12** sand      +      castle      =      _____

**13** snow      +      ball        =      _____    ○ 5

Write these words in the order you find them in a dictionary.

| dog | ant | cat | badger |
|---|---|---|---|

**14** (1) _____      **15** (2) _____

**16** (3) _____      **17** (4) _____    ○ 4

Look at the pictures. Write in the speech bubbles what the children are saying.

**18**                                **19–20**

⟨ 3

## Paper 7

| lorry | a large vehicle that carries loads | **Mm** | |
| **lounge** | a room in a house/ hotel where people sit | **magazine** | a thin book which is usually sold monthly or weekly |
| **low** | (1) close to the ground (2) feeling miserable | **magic** | in stories magic makes impossible things happen |
| **luggage** | things you take with you in suitcases or bags | **mammal** | a warm-blooded animal |
| **lunch** | a meal in the middle of the day | **mane** | long thick hair that grows on the neck of an animal |
| **lynx** | an animal in the cat family | **map** | a drawing from above of a particular area |
| | | **marble** | (1) a type of hard rock that shines when polished (2) a small, coloured glass ball used to play games |

Underline the right answers.

1 How many **M** words are there on this dictionary page?

(5, 6, 7)

2 Which **L** word has two meanings?

(low, lunch, luggage)

Answer these questions.

3 Which word means long thick hair? _____

4–5 Write two things a dictionary can be used for.

(1) _____

(2) _____

2

3

Write these **verbs** in the **past tense** by adding *ed*.

6 jump _____    7 kick _____

8 yell _____    9 walk _____    4

Copy this sentence and add the missing commas.

10–12 Tony bought bread, milk, potatoes, shampoo and sweets at the shop.

_____

_____    3

Write two words ending in *ng* and two words ending in *nk*.

13–14 **ng** _____    _____

15–16 **nk** _____    _____    4

Find the four days of the week hidden in the wordsearch and write them in the spaces below.

| t | h | u | r | s | d | a | y |
|---|---|---|---|---|---|---|---|
| u | f | m | k | y | s | l | o |
| e | q | o | p | o | s | a | p |
| s | u | n | d | a | y | d | n |
| d | o | d | y | w | w | o | d |
| a | f | a | e | k | e | m | u |
| y | r | y | u | s | d | j | y |

17 _____    18 _____

19 _____    20 _____    4

# Paper 8

## Slick Nick's Dog's Tricks

Slick Nick's dog does tricks.
The tricks Nick's dog does are slick.
He picks up sticks, stands on bricks,
Nick's finger clicks, the dog barks SIX!
He picks a mix of doggy bix
then gives Slick Nick thick sloppy licks.
Mick and Rick's dog's not so quick –
kicks the bricks, drops the sticks,
can't bark to six, is in a fix,
gets Mick and Rick to do its tricks,
gets on their wicks despite its mix
of waggy tail and loving licks –
but Slick Nick's dog does tricks.
The tricks Nick's dog does are slick.

By David Harmer

Underline the right answers.

1 How many times does Nick's dog bark?

(four, five, six)

2 What does Mick and Rick's dog do with sticks?

(catches sticks, drops sticks, picks up sticks)

2

Answer these questions.

3 Who does Mick and Rick's dog get to do his tricks?

_____

4 Nick's dog gives him 'sloppy licks'. Write another word for 'sloppy'.

_____

2

Sort the letters to make a *th* word.

**5** h n t i _____

**6** t t h e e _____

**7** r e h t e ___th_____

**8** i k t n h ___th_____

4

Write a **synonym** (a word that has a similar meaning).

**9** fast _____    **10** leap _____

**11** sad _____    **12** ill _____

4

Copy the sentences and add the missing capital letters.

**13** At school i work very hard.

_____

**14–15** i always wash my hands when i have made them dirty.

_____

**16** Meena says i am her best friend.

_____

4

Underline the **proper noun** in each sentence.

**17** My nanny lives in Australia.

**18** My best friend is Alice.

**19** I am going shopping in Stafford.

**20** Imran is coming to my house for tea.

4

## Paper 9

Slowly through the darkness, a dinosaur floated down from space, to my bedroom window. I sat up in bed, and stared as it came closer and closer. It landed in my back garden with a thump. I cautiously got out of bed and crept to the window to get a closer look. It was an Allosaurus! And it was coming my way! I gulped, and tried to run away, but I was frozen to the spot. As it came closer and closer, it seemed to get bigger. The Allosaurus lowered its head and its huge eyes stared at me, hard.

From *2001 – A Space Oddity* by Jenny Dale aged 9

Underline the right answers.

1 Where did the dinosaur land?

(in the bedroom, on the house, in the garden)

2 What size was the dinosaur?

(very small, small, big)

2

Answer these questions.

3 Why do you think the person in the story was 'frozen to the spot'?

_____

_____

4 What do you think might have happened next?

_____

_____

_____

_____

2

How many **consonant letters** are in each of these words?

   **5** elephant _____

   **6** breakfast _____

   **7** Saturday _____

   **8** trombone _____          4

Copy these sentences and add the missing speech marks (" ").

   **9** Where are we going? asked Paula.

   _____

   **10** Come back, called Salima.

   _____

   **11** Time to sit down, said the teacher.

   _____

   **12** What is the time? asked Joseph.

   _____          4

There are four letters missing in this alphabet. Which letters are
they?

   **a  b  c  d  e  f  h  i  j  k  l  n  o  p  r  s  t  u  v  x  y  z**

   **13** _____    **14** _____    **15** _____    **16** _____          4

Add a different **verb** to each of these sentences.

   **17** David _____ towards the swings.

   **18** Ilesh _____ in the muddy puddle.

   **19** Fiona always _____ her dog in the morning.

   **20** The children _____ to be first in the pool.          4

## Paper 10

### Snow

Small snowflakes are formed when the clouds get very cold. Snowflakes are frozen droplets of water that fall from the clouds. Each snowflake has a different pattern. If you catch one on your glove, look closely and you might see the delicate pattern of the snowflake.

Snow can be great fun. Many people enjoy throwing snowballs and building snowmen. In some countries, where there is often a lot of snow, children have their own skis. They ski to school or their friends' houses!

If there is a lot of snow it can cause some problems. It can block roads and railways, which stops people getting to work and school. It can be hard for older people to get out in the snow to do their shopping, as snow can be very slippery to walk on.

 Often birds and wild animals find it difficult to find their food buried under all the snow; and because it is so cold, water freezes and so birds and animals can't easily find water to drink.

Underline the right answers.

**1–2** Why don't some people enjoy the snow?

(they find it hard to walk on, they can play in it, it blocks the railways, they can ski on it)

2

Answer these questions.

**3** Do you enjoy the snow? Why?

_____

_____

_____

**4** When it snows, how can we help the birds and the wild animals?

_____

_____

_____

2

Add *ing* to the word. Then write it in a sentence.

**5–6** sleep  _____

_____

**7–8** jump  _____

_____

**9–10** fall  _____

_____   **6**

Add two more words to each column of the table. The words in each column must rhyme.

**11–16**

| ie words | i–e words | y words |
|----------|-----------|---------|
| *tie* | *smile* | *spy* |
|  |  |  |
|  |  |  |

  **6**

Sort the letters to find the name of a month. Remember to make the first letter a capital letter.

**17** n  j  e  u       _____

**18** u  y  j  n  a  r  a       _____

**19** r  i  a  p  l       _____

**20** r  c  t  o  e  b  o       _____   **4**

One evening in Spring, Hare was dancing along the fields, skipping and tripping and bowing to the rabbits. It was the month of March and he was feeling excited and wild, for all hares are mad in March.

"I'll go to the village," said he. "I'll go and see what there is to be seen and tell them at home all about it. I feel very brave tonight."

He stuck a primrose in his coat for luck and a cowslip in his collar for bravery, and he cut a hazel switch with catkins dangling from it, just in case.

"I'll look at the village shop and see if Mrs Bunting and the shop-bell are still there."

It was dusk when he reached the village and the children were indoors having tea. Not even a dog or cat was to be seen. Hare leapt softly and swiftly down the cobbled street.

He gave a chirrup of joy when he saw that the shop was still open. Jars of sweets in the window shone with many colours in the light of the lamp.

Hare crept close. It was a lovely sight! Whips and tops, dolls and toy horses, cakes and buns were there.

Then he opened his eyes very wide, for he saw something strange. On a dish lay a pile of chocolate eggs with sugary flowers and 'Happy Easter' written on them. Ribbons were tied round them in blue, pink and yellow bows.

"Eggs! 'Normous eggs!" whispered Hare.

He stared and licked his lips.

"What kind of hen lays these pretty eggs? I should like to take Grey Rabbit one, and Squirrel one and me one."

He pressed closer to the glass and his long ears flapped against the pane. Just then footsteps came down the street, and he slipped into the shadows and crouched there dark as night. His fur quivered, and his heart thumped.

From *Hare and the Easter Eggs* by Alison Uttley

Underline the right answers.

1 What did Hare take with him for bravery?

(a primrose, a cowslip, catkins)

2 What did Hare find most interesting in the shop window?

(the sweets, the toy horses, the chocolate eggs)

2

Answer these questions.

**3** When footsteps came down the street Hare was frightened.
Copy the sentence that describes how frightened Hare was.

_____

**4** What do you think happens next in this story?

_____

_____

Add a word from the box to each sentence. Use each word only once.

| then | during | after | before |
|------|--------|-------|--------|

**5** Adam continued to work ____during____ his lunchtime.

**6** Salima dried her hair ____after____ she had washed it.

**7** First Helen washed the dishes ____then____ she dried them.

**8** Janu ate her breakfast ____before____ she left for school.

Add the **suffix** *ly* to these words.

**9** quiet + ly = _____     **10** quick + ly = _____

**11** smart + ly = _____     **12** safe + ly = _____

Copy each sentence and add the missing capital letters and full stops.

**13–14** the children went to the dentist

_____

**15–17** one morning jacob met a strange-looking lizard

_____

Put these words in **alphabetical order**.

    **rubber**       **pencil**       **sharpener**
    2                        3

**18** (1) _____          **19** (2) _____

**20** (3) _____

*Hippo was the strongest of all the animals, so he said he should be Chief. The other animals didn't want Hippo as their Chief. He was too grumpy and moody.*

"I bet I can get you out of the pool, Hippo," called Monkey.

"I bet you can't," grunted Hippo. "I'm the strongest animal in the world."

"If I can get you out of the pool, then I should be Chief," said Monkey.

"If you can get me out of the pool, then you can be Chief," said Hippo, "but if I get you into the pool, you will be my servant – for ever!"

Off went Monkey to get a really strong rope.

"Hold tight to the rope," said Monkey, "but don't pull until I shout."

Monkey ran into the trees with the other end of the rope. All the animals watched. Monkey tied the rope to a big, strong tree trunk.

"Pull!" shouted Monkey. "Pull!"

"This will be easy," thought Hippo to himself.

But all day and all night Hippo pulled, while Monkey sat and ate bananas, and snoozed! Hippo was getting very tired and cross, very cross indeed.

"That monkey must be the strongest monkey I've ever known," thought Hippo.

Slowly he climbed out of the pool, to try to see Monkey.

Just as Hippo took his last foot out of the pool, Monkey ran out of the trees ...

*Hippo and Monkey*, a Nigerian folk tale retold by John Jackman

Underline the right answers.

1 Which animal was the strongest?

(Monkey, Hippo, another animal)

2 When Hippo was pulling the rope, could he see Monkey?

(yes, no)

2

Answer these questions.

**3** Write a description of what Hippo was like.

_____

_____

**4** What do you think Monkey said to Hippo when he ran out of the trees?

_____

_____

2

Sort the letters to find a colour.

**5** b c a l k _____    **6** u p r e l p _____

**7** r o n b w _____    **8** e n e g r _____

4

Finish the sentence below with the things on the list. Don't forget the commas.

**Things to remember:**
towel
drink
swimming costume
brush
money

**9–11** When we went swimming, we had to remember a _____

_____

3

Underline the part of each word that sounds the same.

**12–13** crow    boat    **14–15** toe    blow    **16–17** goat    doe

6

Fill the gaps correctly with *is* or *are*.

**18** Ten children _____ playing on the climbing frame.

**19** Lucy _____ going to Paul's house for tea.

**20** Adele and Tony _____ going on holiday.

3

# Paper 13

**Index**

| | | | |
|---|---|---|---|
| accidents | 12, 27 | grooming | 8 |
| ailments | 3–5 | | |
| | | health | 3, 22 |
| bathing | 28 | hygiene | 23 |
| beds | 14, 16 | | |
| bones | 27 | injuries | 29–30 |
| breed types | 35–36 | | |
| | | kennels | 14 |
| claws | 6 | | |
| collars | 2 | leads | 3 |
| | | | |
| Dalmatians | 35 | mating | 34 |
| | | medicine | 5 |
| ears | 4, 12, 24 | | |
| exercise | 2–3 | nits | 4 |
| eyes | 25 | | |
| | | paws | 2, 10 |
| feeding | 7 | puppies | 35 |
| first aid | 10 | | |
| fleas | 5 | | |

Underline the right answers.

1   On which page of the book would you find out about medicine?

(5, 17, 34)

2   What two subjects can you find out about on page 27?

(bathing and hygiene, Dalmatians and puppies, accidents and bones)

2

Answer these questions.

**3** This index is for a book. What do you think that book is about?

_____

**4** Which letters of the alphabet before 'p' do not have an entry in this index? _____

2

Copy these words into the table below under the subjects you might find them in.

| rod | mixing bowl | dried fruit | maggots |

| waterproof clothing | | oven | |

5–10

| Fishing | Cooking |
|---------|---------|
|  |  |
|  |  |
|  |  |

6

Circle the **pronoun(s)** in each sentence.

**11** Ali passed him the ball.

**12–13** We saw her at the shops.

**14** The scarf looked like hers.

4

Finish the two sentences.

**15** When will _____

**16** What does _____

2

Write two words that begin with *ch*.

**17–18** _____        _____

Write two words that end with *ch*.

**19–20** _____        _____

4

## Paper 14

### The Lion and the Mouse

Beneath the spreading baobab,
the lion slept.

Mouse scuttled over parched earth,
climbed unwittingly the sandy mound
then saw – too late.
Fresh from hungry dreams
the lion awoke
and snatched the mouse.

*Spare me, free me, please!*
begged Mouse.
*Oh, wise and strong and tall,*
*lord of all hunters,*
*king of all creatures;*
*your strength and power are great,*
*my strength is small ...*

*Save me, spare my life, I pray!*
*Though I am weak, I know,*
*I promise that one day*
*I will repay you.*
*Let me go!*

The lion roared with mirth.
*You, repay me?*
*You, one of the smallest on the earth ...?*
*We'll see!*

Yet, shaking still with mirth,
he set him free.

The mouse walked free –
but not the lion.
When next they met
the lion, whimpering in despair,
lay tangled in a hunter's net,
roped to a tree.

*At last, my turn!*
cried grateful Mouse.
*Now I can keep my promise,*
*just you see!*

And patiently he bit and gnawed,
he gnawed and bit until, at last,
the net was opened up:

the lion was free!

By Judith Nicholls

Underline the right answers.

1  Why did the lion grab the mouse?

(he was hungry, he didn't like mice, he wanted to frighten the mouse)

2  What is the lion 'king' of?

(hunters, creatures, all the weak)

2

Answer these questions.

3  How did the mouse repay the lion for setting him free?

_____

_____

4  What message does this poem give us about strong and weak things?

_____

_____

2

Add the missing words to the table.

5–9

| Present tense (happening now) | Past tense (happened in the past) |
|---|---|
| dig | |
| give | |
| say | |
| tell | |
| grow | |

5

Add *ee* or *ea* to spell each word correctly.

10  sl_____p

11  str_____m

12  sh_____p

13  scr_____m

Copy these book titles, adding the missing capital letters.

14  the river thames

_____

15  jack dresses up!

_____

16  dinosaurs in water

_____

Draw lines to match the **antonyms** (words with opposite meanings).

17  clean          open

18  hard           run

19  shut           dirty

20  walk           soft

# Paper 15

| | |
|---|---|
| **ink** | a coloured liquid used for writing and printing |
| **insect** | a small animal with six legs |
| **instrument** | (1) a tool used for a job |
| | (2) something you play to make music |
| **Jj** | |
| **jar** | a container, usually made of glass |
| **jaw** | the lower part of your face, below your mouth |
| **jeans** | trousers made from a strong cotton material |
| **jelly** | a clear food that wobbles |
| **jellyfish** | a creature that lives in the sea and looks a bit like jelly |
| **jerk** | a quick, sudden movement |
| **jet** | a very fast aircraft |
| **jewel** | a precious stone, such as a diamond |
| **jewellery** | the name for ornaments people wear, such as rings and necklaces |

Underline the right answers.

1 What has six legs?

(a jerk, a jellyfish, an insect)

2 Which word has two definitions?

(jewellery, jaw, instrument)

 2

Answer these questions.

3 What is the last word in the dictionary that begins with 'i'?

_____

4 Which word means a sudden movement?

_____

2

Write a question that each statement answers.

Example   Sarah had baked beans for tea.

*What did Sarah have for tea?*

5  Statement: Brian went swimming at 3 o'clock.

_____

6  Statement: Alice went to Mark's house for tea.

_____

7  Statement: Mum wore a red jumper on Tuesday.

_____

8  Statement: The school fête is on 16th May.

_____  **4**

Add the **suffix** *ful* to these words.

9  help     + ful  =  _____

10  pain    + ful  =  _____

11  care    + ful  =  _____

12  wonder + ful  =  _____  **4**

Write these words in **alphabetical order**.

**walk**        **swim**        **run**        **crawl**

13 (1) _____    14 (2) _____

15 (3) _____    16 (4) _____  **4**

Underline the **proper noun** in each sentence.

17  Yasmin enjoyed swimming.

18  We went to Birmingham.

19  Jess lives in a caravan.

20  I went to visit my grandparents in India.  **4**

# Paper 16

*George had just started school. At the beginning of the week he was in the reception class, by the end he was in Year 6. George was a very talented child, in fact he was top of the top class. At the end of his first week at school he went to bed saying he felt tired ... suddenly there was an awful wailing coming from his bedroom.*

"I'm coming, my baby!" called George's mother. "Mummy's coming!" and she rushed upstairs to find George sitting up in bed, sobbing his heart out. This was not the confident self-assured know-it-all cleverest child in the school. This was just a frightened baby, and she cuddled him as fiercely as she had when he was only tiny and had never spoken a word. "What is it, George darling?" she said as she mopped away his tears. "Did you have a bad dream?"

"I did, I did Mummy!" sobbed George.

"What was it? Tell Mummy."

Gradually George's sobs turned to sniffles, and then he blew his nose and said, "I dreamt we were doing a science test at school."

"A science test?"

"Yes, we do science in the new curriculum, you know. And there was a simple question in it that I couldn't answer, and I cried like a baby. I cried in the dream, and I was crying when I woke up. I really must apologise for behaving so childishly."

"Poor lamb!" said his mother. "What was the question?"

"It was the order of events in the cycle of the internal combustion engine," said George.

"Forget about it, George," said his mother sadly. "I expect that there'll be lots of questions you won't know the answers to."

"Not if I can help it," said George.

"Anyway, don't worry. Just go back to sleep. Mummy's here."

"Oh, I shan't worry any more, Mother," said George in his usual confident tones. "I've remembered it now. It's Induction – Compression – Ignition – Exhaust," and exhausted, he lay back and went happily to sleep.

From *George Starts School* by Dick King-Smith

Underline the right answers.

1 What test did George dream about?

   (maths test, spelling test, science test)

2 Why did George apologise to his mother?

   (for not knowing the answer, for waking up, for behaving childishly)

Answer these questions.

3–4 Write two words that could be used to describe George.

   _____     _____

5–6 Write two reasons why you think George was exhausted when 'he lay back and went happily to sleep'.

   (1) _____

   (2) _____

Write the **plural** of each of these words.

   7 boot _____        8 jumper _____

   9 farm _____        10 lamp _____

Add the missing commas to this sentence.

11–12 The horse jumped over the gate the hay bale Jacob's bike and then escaped onto the road.

Underline the **verb** in each of these sentences.

   13 Fiona swam for forty minutes.

   14 Tuhil kicked his ball hard.

   15 The ducklings waddled onto the grass.

   16 Lara lost her homework.

2

2

2

4

2

4

Write these sentences in the correct order.

**Then he found the robe he lost last year.**

**Once upon a time a king lost his crown.**

**In the end he found his crown; he had left it in the bathroom!**

**While he was searching he found his glasses.**

17 (1) _____

_____

18 (2) _____

_____

19 (3) _____

_____

20 (4) _____

_____ ◯ 4

## Paper 17

**The Life Cycle of a Frog**

A frog lays some eggs.

The egg is protected by a jelly-like material.

The tail-bud begins to grow.

The tadpole wriggles free and attaches to some weed.

The back legs begin to grow.

Then the front legs grow.

After about eleven weeks the frog

is fully grown and can leave the water.

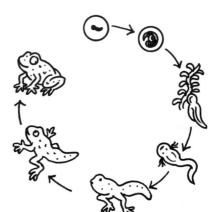

Underline the right answers.

1 What is the egg protected by?

(the frog, pond weed, a jelly-like material)

2 Which legs grow first?

(the front legs, the back legs)

2

Answer these questions.

3 About how many weeks does it take an egg to grow into a frog?

_____

4 Why do you think the tadpole attaches to some weed when it leaves the jelly-like material?

_____

_____

2

Write a word with *ai* or *ay* to match each picture.

5 _____

6 _____

7 _____

8 _____

○ 4

Write a question sentence starting with each of these words.

9 Where _____

10 When _____

11 What _____

12 Which _____

○ 4

Find the four words in the wordsearch and write them in the spaces.

Clue: each word can be found in a classroom.

13–16

| t | r | o | l | p | x | a | g |
|---|---|---|---|---|---|---|---|
| g | t | e | a | c | h | e | r |
| p | a | i | n | t | l | b | j |
| s | b | d | u | r | p | o | r |
| w | l | h | y | r | s | o | s |
| z | e | g | j | r | u | k | m |

_____

_____

_____

_____

○ 4

Write each of these words in a sentence.

17 before

_____

18 next

_____

19 during

_____

20 meanwhile

_____

○ 4

# Paper 18

**Magic Cat**

My mum whilst walking through the door
Spilt some magic on the floor.
Blobs of this
and splots of that
but most of it upon the cat.

Our cat turned magic, straight away
and in the garden went to play
where it grew two massive wings
and flew around in fancy rings.
'Oh look!' cried Mother, pointing high,
'I didn't know our cat could fly.'
Then with a dash of Tibby's tail
she turned my mum into a snail!
So now she lives beneath a stone
and dusts around a different home.
And I'm an ant
and Dad's a mouse
And Tibby's living in our house.

By Peter Dixon

Underline the right answers.

1 What did the cat grow when the magic spilt on her?

(big wings, big whiskers, a big tail)

2 Who lives in the house at the end of the poem?

(Dad, the snail, the cat)

2

Answer these questions.

3 Find a word in the poem that means the same as 'under'.

_____

4 Do you think Tibby liked having the magic spilt on her? Why?

_____

_____

2

Copy these book titles, adding the missing capital letters.

**5** school stories

_____          _____

**6** the badger's bath

_____

**7** famous people in history

_____

**8** growing a sunflower

_____          4

Add the **prefix** _dis_ to each word to make its **antonym**.

**9** _____like          **10** _____obey

**11** _____appear          **12** _____trust          4

Write three words you would use to write about each of these topics.

**13** school      _____    _____    _____

**14** football    _____    _____    _____

**15** weddings  _____    _____    _____

**16** art         _____    _____    _____          4

Fill each gap with a word in the **present tense**. Use the words in bold
to help. Use each word only once.

**Example**      The boy is walking.      **walk**

**17** The cats are _____.          **fight**

**18** Jake is _____ his ruler.          **bend**

**19** The boys are _____ the ball.          **throw**

**20** Aimee is _____ her Dad.          **help**          4

# Paper 19

## Faces

Look in the mirror. Which part of your body do you see? Probably, your face. This is the most-looked-at part of anybody's body, for many reasons.

Faces are truly fascinating. They show people's moods – happy, sad, pleased, worried, tired or thoughtful. Tiny movements of the eyebrows and eyelids can mean a lot, like surprise or anger. A flicker around the lips may mean that a smile is coming, or a frown.

In most countries a nod of the head indicates yes, and a shake means no.

When we listen to people speak, we also watch the movements of their mouths and lips. This helps us to make out what they say. Also, the rest of the body is often covered by clothes, so you cannot see it!

## How faces change with age

As you grow, your face gets bigger. It also changes its proportions. A baby's face is small compared to the size of its whole head. Its eyes and forehead are big, its nose and mouth are small. In a grown-up, the nose and mouth take up more of the face. And the face takes up more than half of the front of the head.

From *Learn about the Body* by Steve Parker

Underline the right answers.

1 In most countries, what does a shake of the head mean?

(yes, no)

2 What feature is small on a baby's face?

(eyes, nose, forehead)

2

Answer these questions.

**3** Write another mood your face might show that isn't listed above.

_____

**4** Give a reason why your face is the most-looked-at part of your body.

_____  ◯ 2

Circle a **noun** and underline a **verb** in each sentence.

**5–6** The dog swam in the river.

**7–8** We ate some sweets.

**9–10** They jumped onto the wall.  ◯ 6

Only copy the words which have been said.

**11** "We must put our coats on," said Hannah.

_____

**12** "Where is my hat?" asked Nazar.

_____

**13** "It is cold outside," warned Jack.

_____  ◯ 3

Solve the clues using a _wh_ or _ph_ word from the box.

| elephant | dolphin | wheel | white |
|---|---|---|---|

**14** I am grey and swim. _____

**15** I help things move from one place to another. _____

**16** I am very big and usually live in hot places. _____

**17** I am a colour. _____  ◯ 4

Write a **synonym** for each word.

**18** quick _____      **19** chew _____

**20** shout _____  ◯ 3

### The Owl and the Pussy-Cat

The Owl and the Pussy-Cat went to sea
In a beautiful pea-green boat,
They took some honey, and plenty of money,
Wrapped up in a five-pound note.
The Owl looked up to the stars above,
And sang to a small guitar,
'O lovely Pussy! O Pussy, my love,
What a beautiful Pussy you are,
You are,
You are!
What a beautiful Pussy you are!'

Pussy said to the Owl, 'You elegant fowl!
How charmingly sweet you sing!
O let us be married! too long have we tarried:
But what shall we do for a ring?'
They sailed away for a year and a day,
To the land where the Bong-tree grows,
And there in a wood a Piggy-wig stood
With a ring at the end of his nose,
His nose,
His nose,
With a ring at the end of his nose.

'Dear Pig, are you willing to sell for one shilling
Your ring?' Said the Piggy, 'I will.'
So they took it away, and were married next day
By the Turkey who lives on the hill.
They dined on mince and slices of quince,
Which they ate with a runcible spoon;
And hand in hand, on the edge of the sand,
They danced by the light of the moon,
The moon,
The moon,
They danced by the light of the moon.

By Edward Lear

Underline the right answers.

I For how much did the Piggy-wig sell his ring?

(one shilling, five shillings, five pounds)

**2** Where does the Turkey live?

(on the beach, on the hill, in a wood)

2

Answer these questions.

**3** Why did the Owl and the Pussy-Cat want the Piggy's ring?

_____

_____

**4** Which verse of this poem do you like the best? Why?

_____

_____

_____

2

Put these words in **alphabetical order**.

**pizza**          **curry**          **sausages**          **mushrooms**

**5** (1) _____          **6** (2) _____

**7** (3) _____          **8** (4) _____

4

Copy and add the missing punctuation to each sentence.

**9–11** Please come to my house for tea said Clare

_____

**12–14** When shall I come to tea asked Jess

_____

6

Underline the part of each word that sounds the same.

**15–17** bird          purse          nerve

3

Circle the **pronouns** in these sentences.

**18** I went to the shop.          **19** They ate bananas.

**20** Can we go swimming?

3

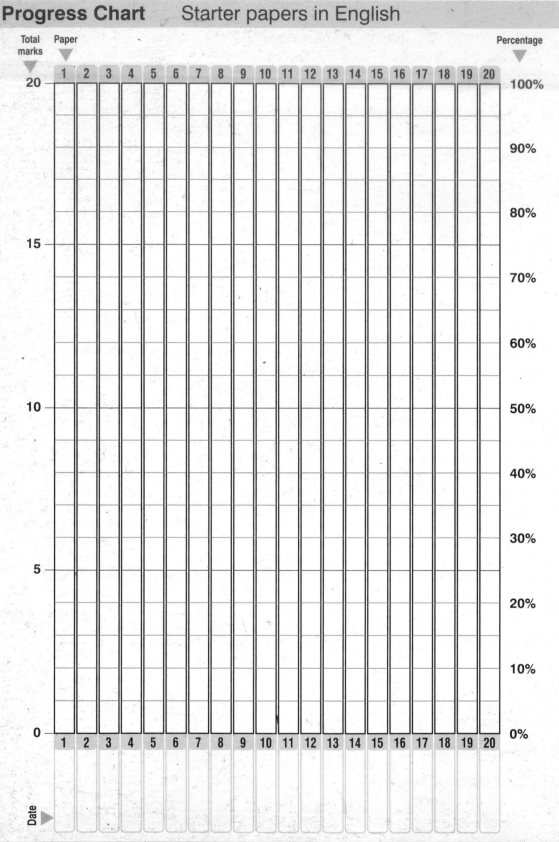

# Progress Chart    Starter papers in English